Dealing with Divas

Dealing with Divas

A Survivor's Kit for the Celebrity Personal Assistant (Or Anyone with a Pushy Boss)

SHELLEY ANDERSON

iUniverse, Inc.
New York Lincoln Shanghai

Dealing with Divas

A Survivor's Kit for the Celebrity Personal Assistant (Or Anyone with a Pushy Boss)

iUniverse books may be ordered through booksellers or by contacting:

iUniverse
2021 Pine Lake Road, Suite 100
Lincoln, NE 68512
www.iuniverse.com
1-800-Authors (1-800-288-4677)

ISBN: 978-0-595-43436-7 (pbk)
ISBN: 978-0-595-87763-8 (ebk)

Printed in the United States of America

For April Genet

To know the road ahead, ask those coming back.
—Chinese proverb

Contents

Acknowledgments

I could not have done this book without iUniverse and Brenda Kluck. Special thanks also go to the following people for their unending emotional support while I was writing this book: Linda Bounds, Barbara Carrellas, Terah Kathryn Collins, Kathleen Dennish, Victoria Guasco, Barbara Hariston, David M. Huffman, Marcie Hintz, Mark Husson, R. Dean Johnson, the Levy family, Kimberly Logan, Pattee Mack, Gary Potter, Loria Roberson, Jo'Ann Ruhl, Linda Schilling, Enid Unatin, Judy Weber, J. W. Winston, and celebrity personal assistants everywhere. Bless you all!

Introduction

It's a quiet, spring afternoon in San Diego. I'm at home enjoying the day. The phone rings.

"Hi. I'm returning your call." It's my employer, author Louise L. Hay.

"What do you mean you're returning my call?" I ask.

"Well, I looked at my cell phone and it was beeping, so I noticed I had a call and it was from you."

It takes me a moment to understand what happened. Then I respond, "Louise. That call—the one you say I made to you?—was from two and a half years ago."

"What?"

"Yes, remember when you first got the cell phone you said, 'call me and leave a message so I can figure out how to get my calls?' Well, that's the call."

"Ohh. Never mind."

Louise loves technology, but only if the manual to deal with it is at her fingertips. And that "manual" would be me! I'm her personal assistant—the person who manages her office, her schedule, her travel, and her home.

When I was growing up, I didn't dream about being a celebrity personal assistant; I dreamed about being a princess or a ballerina. Okay, I grew to be almost six feet tall, so the dance career choice wasn't the right one. But I could dream, yes?

How did I get here, and why am I writing a book about it? My story really begins in 1988. It's ten o'clock in the morning, and I'm dressed head to toe in a sexy black dress and high-heeled shoes on my way to an audition callback appointment for the Broadway-bound musical, *Nine.* At the audition, the producers love my operatic voice and my command of Italian, but, alas, I do not get the part.

Afterward, I went directly from the audition to my job as the assistant to a film producer. I sat at my desk—still in my black cocktail dress, the bright Southern California sun streaming through the window—and thought to myself, who am I kidding? I'd been singing and working as a professional actress for over twenty years, and I was tired. Tired of the auditions, tired of ordering new eight-by-ten-inch glossy photos every year—tired of it all. Maybe it was time to give that all up and focus on my multitasking administrative skills instead.

So I opened up the Help Wanted section of the *Los Angeles Times*. There, in a black-bordered box, was this job ad: "Executive Secretary needed for President of Angel Records. Contact HR at Capitol-EMI Records if interested." This little ad was about to change my life.

As an opera and classical music student, I had long been a fan of Angel Records and knew that that label was the epitome of professional achievement for classical musicians. If you recorded for Angel Records, you were a bona fide star. Celebrities on this label included Itzhak Perlman, Beverly Sills, Placido Domingo, and eventually Andrew Lloyd Webber. Plus, the Capitol label had such infamous pop stars as Frank Sinatra, Tina Turner, and even The Beatles! I responded to the ad enthusiastically, and one week later I was working for the president of Angel Records in the historic round Capitol Records building at Hollywood and Vine. Wow.

During my eight years at Capitol-EMI Records, I interacted with many musicians and their assistants, agents, producers, and go-betweens on a daily basis. I formed close friendships with the stars, and often with their people behind the scenes. This environment allowed me to use my creative skills and organizational abilities to their fullest. Often I had to think on my feet to make sure a star was taken care of when plans changed at the last moment. I found out very quickly that not only was I good at what I did, but I actually enjoyed the variety. Each day was an adventure.

Fast forward to 1998. I'd moved from Los Angeles to San Diego and once again was reading the Help Wanted ads. It was just like a decade ago: there, in a black-bordered box, was this ad: "Personal Assistant to author Louise L. Hay needed as soon as possible." I faxed my resume to the number requested in the ad, along with a cover letter that simply stated: *I know how to work with divas. Call me.* Louise did, and I've worked for her ever since. Little did I know that all those years at Capitol-EMI Records had prepared me for this new career. However, I did know one thing: if I could work with touchy opera stars, I could work for anyone.

One thing I want you to know about celebrity personal assistants is that there's no set formula to be one. We come from all walks of life—all races, all professions, and both sexes. Yes, there are male celebrity personal assistants! I would say the vast majority of assistants are women; maybe 85 percent. But not to take anything away from the male assistants out there: the guys I know in this business are fantastic at it!

What sets a celebrity personal assistant's job apart from other personal assistants or office staff—if that's what you want to call us—is that we do a variety of odd tasks; everything from having the employer's dogs nails trimmed to planning a birthday party for his children with only six hours notice. Often our jobs require us to never sit still for more than a few minutes at a time because we're interacting with so many different people all day long. It's not unusual, for instance, to spend half a day outside of the office environment taking the employer's car in for service, picking up an employer's relative at the airport, or meeting a representative from the Academy of Motion Picture Arts and Sciences under a freeway passage to get ticket to the Oscars (I actually had to do that once!). Perhaps that's why I like my job—it's constantly changing. Each day is different from the next.

On a typical workday, I might send out personal letters and checks to my employer's favorite charities and causes, then arrange for her to be taken to the airport for a trip, while giving last-minute instructions to the housekeeper about food shopping while the boss is away. The next day, we could have a proofreading deadline on a marketing catalog sent over from her publishing house to be returned on the same day if possible; then lunch with a famous author who just happens to be in town and wants to catch up with us; and also various calls to people like a handyman, to repair something at the house. Two days later, we could be preparing for the makeup and hair artist, then setting up an interview and photo shoot while making sure a friend's dog has a treat packed in the celebrity's handbag when she goes to visit him. Who knows what a day will bring? I love it. The variety is ten times more than what I had at the record label, and I loved my job at Capitol-EMI. It really prepared me to step into the personal assistant arena.

Until I met the members of the ACPA through an article I read in *Vanity Fair*—the Association of Celebrity Personal Assistants—in 2001, I had no idea that being a personal assistant was an actual job category. I thought I was the only one! Since I began working as the personal assistant to author and self-help guru Louise L. Hay, I've learned that there are thousands of people like me in this unique world doing this unique kind of job. Being able to network monthly in Los Angeles at ACPA meetings has been a saving grace for me and my sanity. I am honored to call many of its members my friends. We sometimes kid each other that our monthly meetings should really be called therapy sessions! Due to the confidential nature of the work we do, it has been a comfort to be able to speak freely with each other about the highs and lows of our jobs, knowing that there will be no breach of trust.

What began as a speech for a monthly ACPA meeting on job satisfaction has now been expanded into the book you have in your hands. In 2003, the ACPA asked me to explain why so many of us in this business woke every morning and asked ourselves, "What was I thinking? Why am I dealing with divas all day?" After working in the entertainment industry, first as a performer and vocal coach for years, then as the assistant to the head of a major record company, a film producer, a booking agent, and at a repertory theatre company (among other jobs), I realized that I might have some tools I could offer to my fellow celebrity personal assistants—a survival kit to help them cope, as I've been able to cope, with the stresses of the job. As an advice columnist from 2003 to 2005 for the now-defunct newsletter, *The Right Hand,* I received letters from many assistants who had concerns about their work environment. I heard everything from the mundane to the bizarre. I'm sharing those letters with you in Part Two of this book.

I realize that if you have no experience within this type of working environment, you might be saying to yourself, "What's the big deal? They work for famous people with tons of money. Why are they whining?" Actually, this book will encourage you *not* to whine about life.

But there has to be a starting point. I've noticed that the personal assistants who've asked for my humble advice on all matters celebrity have actually made significant changes in their working lives—as well as their personal lives—by using my L.A.R.K. method. I believe it works, so I am sharing it with you. I know it has worked in my life.

I offer this book to all celebrity personal assistants and anyone in a service industry job as a survival guide. If you truly want to have a better working environment and would like to see positive changes happen in all areas of your life, I recommend you give my L.A.R.K. method a try. What can it hurt? Go for it! I also hope that if you are just one of the many curious readers who want the inside scoop on Hollywood and the world of celebrity personal assistants that you enjoy what I have to offer. Unfortunately, you'll be disappointed if you're looking for tabloid dirt about the hottest celebrity flavor of the month (depicted in such recent novels as *The Devil Wears Prada* or *Adventures of a Chore Whore*). That's not what this book is about.

Speaking of celebrities, I want to take this moment to acknowledge my wonderful and very supportive employer and friend, author Louise L. Hay. For the past nine-plus years, she has shown me with her kindness that it is possible to work as a celebrity personal assistant and actually be treated as an equal. My life is richer for having known and worked with her. Louise's ability to see the best in me when I didn't always feel I was in prime shape emotionally, mentally, or spiritually has been a huge inspiration. Thank you, Louise!

Finally, I wish anyone who is reading this the same supportive working environment that I've been showered with. If it can happen for me, it can for you, too!

Shelley Anderson
California, 2007

Part One

Chapter One
Riding the Seesaw of Life

Do you sometimes wake up in the morning and say to yourself, "What was I thinking?"

You're not alone. We all have those moments from time to time. "What was I thinking signing on for a 24/7 job?" "What was I thinking when I said I would skip my bridal shower so I could help out at my employer's kid's birthday party?" "What was I thinking driving an hour one way to work every day?" I venture to guess that many people have similar thoughts to these as they prepare for their days. It's such a shame that the first thought of one's day is something negative! But it's not that unusual. Why? Because just trying to survive the seesaw of our lives appears to be normal to many of us.

The word seesaw, as defined by *Webster's New Twentieth Century Dictionary, 2nd Ed, New York, NY: Simon & Schuster, 1983*, literally means: "to lean suddenly or unsteadily from the vertical axis." In other words, you slant from either a vertical or horizontal position. Depending on what you do and where you sit, the seesaw starts to slant. Unless there's some*one* or some*thing* on the other side, the seesaw is unbalanced and has no choice but to move, one way or the other.

Let's look at the two sides of the seesaw. In the table below, Seat A refers to negative thoughts one could have about one's job, and Seat B is the positive outlook. I chose a seesaw because everyone has positive and negative feelings, back and forth—the goal is to just try to have the good outweigh the bad.

SEESAW SEAT A	SEESAW SEAT B
• I don't like my boss.	• My boss admires my work.
• My boss doesn't like me.	• I respect and appreciate my boss.
• I feel depressed when I'm at work.	• I work in a happy and healthy environment.
• No one understands or appreciates me or what I do.	• I'm a compassionate person.
• I regret ever taking this job.	• I'm valued for my abilities and creativity.
• Coworkers dump their workloads on me.	• I love to go to work.
• I'm afraid to speak my mind.	• I find myself empowered in the workplace.
• I feel sick by the end of the day.	• My opinion matters.
• Maybe I don't deserve to get a pay raise.	• My job is fun!
• It's all drudgery and no fun.	• My salary is great.
• My boss doesn't trust me.	• The rewards at work come in many forms.
• It's hopeless to look for another job.	• If I make a mistake, all is forgiven.
	• Each day is a new day filled with mutual respect.

There were times early in my career when I had the low self-esteem described in seesaw seat A. When I first began working at Capitol-EMI Records, many famous classical music artists came into our offices, and I was timid as a mouse. Anyone who knows me now would laugh to hear that, as now I am anything but timid! But I was in such awe of the history of the company, the building, and the people. I couldn't believe that I was now part of that history, too. I allowed people to treat me like a doormat. In the beginning of my tenure there, many people traipsed in and out of my boss's office all day long, and I was never introduced. It was as if I was invisible: a painting on the wall. It was humiliating and embarrassing, and I allowed it to happen for way too long. Over time I realized that I needed to believe in myself and my abilities and to speak up for myself.

Back to the seesaws—if you're relating to seat B, you have a great job. But if you're relating more to seat A, you're most likely experiencing unhappiness in the workplace like I did. What can be done to make your life better? How can you fix this?

When you look at a seesaw, you see it's an object with an obvious slant. But a slant is just an approach. Slanting is how we approach or look at a situation. On this emotional playground we call life, it's good to take a moment to look at whether we are swinging and playing on the monkey bars, or sitting in the sandbox eating mud pies. Which scenario would describe where you are right now in your job and your life?

Life is all about choice. We really do have a choice about how our lives are going at every moment. Often it just takes slowing down. I strongly suggest you take a look at the choices you're making in your life. Perhaps just reading this book is a step in the right direction for you.

Here's a story about choice. A student went to live in a monastery. One of the rules of the monastery was that the students had to take a vow of silence to live there. But, once every ten years, the students were allowed to meet with the head monk and speak one sentence to him.

So the student of our story spends his first ten years in silence. The time comes to meet the head monk and say his one sentence. He goes to the monk and says, "The bed is hard." The monk smiles, and the student goes back to the monastery to study and pray.

Ten more years go by. Again the student meets the monk and he says, "The food is lousy." The monk smiles, and the student returns to the monastery. Now it's thirty years later. Thirty years! The student meets with the monk and says, "I quit!" And the monk replies, "I'm not surprised. You've had a bad attitude since the first day you came here."

This story just goes to show that life is all about your point of view. The monk was just waiting for the student to quit, and the student was putting up with a less-than-ideal environment until he finally couldn't take it anymore.

How each of us feels and reacts throughout each day—throughout our entire lives, really—is what truly counts, not the story. Whining and moaning and groaning and being a victim is no fun for anyone to hear about. Okay, I concede that people *do* like to read personal stories about celebrities. I guess that's why so many magazines like *Entertainment Weekly*, *Us*, and *People* as well as nightly TV shows like *Showbiz Tonight*, *Access Hollywood*, *E! TV,* and all the rest do so well. Maybe people like to live vicariously through the celebrities they meet in the stories they read. If this interests you, I recommend a terrific book entitled *Fame Junkies*, by Jake Halpern. Released by Houghton-Mifflin early in 2007, it looks at the dark side of fame and examines why the general public is obsessed with celebrities and their lives.

However, this book is geared more toward people already working in the entertainment or services industries. Whether you're a butler, nanny, estate manager, or personal assistant, I think this book has something to offer you. In the pages that follow, I'll be offering you hands-on techniques on how to deal with bullying bosses, unreasonable requests, impossible deadlines, and other problems often encountered by assistants and service workers of all kinds. Whether you're working for a high-powered and picky executive, an intense and needy artiste, or a demanding client in any service business, these tips can help you manage your job.

As a personal assistant, I found myself asking all the questions on the pages to follow. After working for a celebrity for a while you may realize that you have stories you *could* tell about your celebrity that would definitely sell a lot of magazines. After the initial excitement of working for a celebrity wears off, you're faced with the reality: first, you know that you won't betray your employer's trust just to help someone sell a magazine; and second, you know you have to get up and go to work every day.

Chapter Two
Sink or Swim

The expression *sink or swim* is one way of looking at the world we work in, albeit with a distrusting eye. If we do what we're told and don't go against the current, we may eventually feel we're drowning. Why? Because doubting our abilities and having lowered self-esteem sinks us deeper and deeper into depression.

While working as an advice columnist, I was shocked at how many people had been working unhappily as celebrity personal assistants for years, feeling that they had no way to change their circumstances. They continued to go to work every day as if they were treading water, certain that if they didn't follow the rules, they would drown. Many were sure that they would never work again or make enough money to survive if they left their celebrity jobs in pursuit of their personal dreams. While it may appear that a person is swimming along fine in their job, secretly they feel they're drowning. So in this case it's really *sink* **and** *swim.*

A general complaint may go something like this: "I go out on interviews on my lunch break to see if I can get hired in a normal office environment—a regular nine-to-five job. But the pay is so bad or I am considered too old or they want computer skills I never learned. I am scared that if I leave my present job, I will never get paid a decent salary again."

I ask, "But aren't you unhappy working for an egomaniac that makes you work from six in the morning until nine at night?" "Yes," is the reply, "but he pays for my cell phone, my laptop, and I even have a gas card. And I went on vacation for two weeks with him to Ireland. Who else is going to give me that?" (It's not just celebrity personal assistants that suffer from many of these problems—being unhappy in a job but seemingly stuck with no choice.)

I often hear people say, "I have no choice." People also like to say, "I can't make a choice." I don't understand either concept. The act of not choosing *is* a choice! Thinking you have no choice in your life may not *feel* good. You might have a lot of emotion tied up in feeling there's no hope, no way out. The entertainment industry perpetuates the myth that "this is the way it's always been done, so don't rock the boat." Many traditional, corporate environments send their employees this same, negative message.

We have nothing in our lives but choice. Here's a look at daily choices we might have:

Get up early in the morning or stay in bed an extra few minutes?
Take a shower or don't?
Stay in the shower or get out?
Get dressed or go back to sleep?
If dressing, what to wear?
Eat something or not?
Decaf or regular?
Go to work or not?
Complain or not?
Forgive or not?
Speak up or not?

The list of choices, as you can see, is endless.

Feeling trapped and not able to make choices in your life is really all about fear—fear of the consequences of what would happen if you *do* make a choice. This isn't something that just happened to you yesterday. This fear of making a choice seems very real and has a grip on all of us due to conditioning beginning in our youths. It feels very real—as real as the difference between swimming with the tide and sinking to the bottom of the ocean.

Where does this fear come from? Here are some thoughts:

Let's look at an example of a fearful person. Let's call her Jill. Jill might've been verbally or physically abused as a child. At five years old, she was bullied on the playground. That made Jill begin to feel unworthy. In grade school, Jill spoke up and was laughed at. Fear began to set in. She thought to herself, maybe my choices aren't good enough for other people. In high school, Jill had self-image issues. I'm too tall, too short, fat, skinny, the brainiest in my class.

Jill became a young adult and was spurned by her first encounter with love, convincing her that she was unlovable. She got a job and was underpaid and undervalued. She spoke up and got shot down. She learned again that maybe her opinions didn't really matter.

Given the scenarios described above, some people who have had these events happen in their lives, unfortunately, suffer from low self-esteem. It isn't a very big surprise. In fact, I'm sure you know people, just as I do, in the workplace (or even outside of work, such as family and friends) who are unhappy due to lack of confidence in themselves. It's all about the fear of not being good enough.

Take this fear into your workplace and here's what you have:

- Loss of dignity
- Feeling overworked
- Resenting your boss
- Creating illness in your body
- Lack of integrity
- Loss of pride

In the case of the entertainment industry—the world of celebrity personal assistants in particular, but also in most corporate service environments—the unwritten credos everyone knows are:

- The celebrity/boss/customer is always right. You're only here to serve them.
- The boss is to be served at all costs, even if his or her demands put the job area into chaos.
- Don't be different or stand out.
- Never display your true emotions.
- Make a mistake and you'll pay for it.

- Never trust anyone.
- Work involves long hours and low pay.
- There is a "dog-eat-dog" attitude.
- Work is everything. Your life is nothing.
- Appearance, above all else, is more important than reality or substance.
- Be nice—no matter what.

Probably the most famous credo that anyone in the job world has heard is: "The customer is always right." For anyone reading this who works in a service-oriented industry, such as a housekeeper, waiter, butler, estate manager, or even a customer representative, those words probably make you cringe. I've never understood why some people—the bosses and customers of this world—lose all sense of common courtesy when addressing a personal assistant or service person. They often act as though the person serving them is someone lesser than them, treating the person without dignity.

Follow the above credos and supposedly you'll be successful in the business—or will you? What will be left of the real *you*, as a person, when five, ten, or fifteen years have gone by? The next chapter gives you some tools on how to survive this brutal business mentality and come out ahead.

Chapter Three
Taking the Plunge

What do I mean by "take the plunge"? Just what it sounds like! It's time to get your feet wet. Time to get off the fence. Time to change your life. To "take the plunge," the first step is to stop doing and thinking negatively over and over and to start expecting your job—or your life—to be different. It's time to look at your life in a new way. The common entertainment industry mantra, which sells a lot of magazines and books, is "It's all about me." But when you think of *me* in the world of celebrities, you are actually thinking of *them*. Outside the entertainment industry, employers also often have this same "greater than thou" attitude toward their employees.

In other words, you are most likely working for an employer that considers him or herself to be more powerful in the world than you. For instance, celebrities may read about themselves in the press, and the press tells them, "You are loved by so many fans. You are admired for what you do in the world. You are special. You are handsome. Everyone wants to be you. You are rich. You are different."

In this book, when I say *me*, I am talking about *you*, the reader—not your employer. Who is the most important person in the workplace? If you said Brad Pitt or Rupert Murdoch or your company's head of accounting's name, you're wrong. The most important person in the workplace is you!

Take a deep breath. Look in a mirror, if you can, and say three times:

The most important person at my workplace is me.

Now, do you believe it? Are you looking to others for approval? Do you continually give your power away by putting others ahead, at your own great expense while at work by worrying about what other people think about you, and what you're doing?

Are you a star in your own movie? Or are you a victim, a martyr? It's time to admit that you're human! You make mistakes. We all do.

When I worked as a booking agent for the Los Angeles Unified School system in the late 1970s (scheduling artists to appear in school assemblies in order to showcase their crafts to students), I learned through trial and error about booking people on the wrong day or time, or at the wrong location. For example, before we put the schedules into a computerized system, everything was done by hand, so mix-ups were just waiting to happen. I remember sending an entire band of Hispanic puppeteers very early in the morning to a school that was already setting up their auditorium for a different performing group ... which had been sent by my office also. All of these artists relied on the pay they would receive for each performance they gave, so obviously, on that day, one group was going to be paid and one wasn't. Oops! It was all a learning process, and my patient and understanding boss gave me the leeway to make those rookie mistakes. This goes to show you, even if you make a mistake, it isn't the end of the world. Don't feel like you have to be flawless, because *nobody* is.

Additionally, comparing oneself to everyone around is a bad idea because different people have different abilities, strengths, etc. Therefore, if someone outperforms you in some area, it isn't necessarily because you're stupid, foolish, or anything like that. You may simply be less experienced, so don't beat yourself up.

One of the ways people give their power away is to talk down to themselves. Don't ever say, "I'm stupid." Trust yourself to do the right thing. Know that you're doing the best that you can right now given the knowledge you have at this moment in time. In fact, everyone is just doing the best they can.

The most important person in the workplace is me. Now—believe it!

How do we begin to take the plunge and change our lives? Remember those unwritten credos that we reviewed in Chapter Two? The first step to breaking away from those credos and making them have less effect on one's self-esteem is to change your thinking. Here are some ideas on how to turn a few of those negatives into positives:

 # 1—Old Thought: The celebrity/boss/customer is always right.

If your boss has ten lousy qualities (in your humble opinion) and one wonderful quality, choose the one that is fantastic to put your attention upon. If he or she has ten great traits and one that drives you crazy, don't let that drive you crazy. I know this is easier said than done. Of course, if this negative behavior trait appears to involve something illegal or obviously unethical, such as illegal drug use, I assume you'll get help handling that by bringing in the proper authorities. Asking people around the boss like the spouse, adult children, or business manager, to help is always a good idea. Don't try to do anything on your own! I know we walk a fine line. Sometimes assistants and others work in a unique environment where money and temptations run high.

If you are not in a situation where your life or the lives of people you work with are in danger, or one in which illegal activities are taking place, my guess is that your day-to-day routine with your employer is not super-dramatic. However, I can guarantee that he or she has personality traits that can drive you up a wall. Often employees are walked all over and not treated with respect. This, unfortunately, is all too common in the work place. An occasional unreasonable demand from the employer can be overlooked. But when he or she continues to ask of you what you deem over the top behavior, it might be hard for you to speak up for fear of losing your job. In fact, I know many people who don't speak up exactly for this reason.

I once knew a celebrity who had a bird that flew around the house and home office unattended to. The bird was trained to leave a "prize" in the office wastebasket on a regular basis. All this was so the employer could use the bird's shit for his organic garden. The boss demanded that the assistant be responsible for handing this over to him at the end of every workday. I dare say this is not typical in most workplaces that I am aware of! What a lovely office environment that must've been!

New Thought: I won't rehash the past or place blame, resentment, anger, or guilt on my employer for past abuses. Instead, today I focus on the aspects of this person's personality that I like and think of those while I'm working for them.

 # 2—Old Thought: The boss is to be served at all costs, even if his or her demands put the job area in chaos.

Communication is so important. I often find that if I let the celebrity know that they are being too demanding and thus sacrificing one thing for another, they'll listen to reason and hear options. For instance, is taking the boss to the mall more important than waiting for the roof repairmen to arrive to begin to demolish the roof? Sometimes, it may seem impossible to you to actually get your employer to listen for a moment. Confront your boss in front of a witness if you have to—grab the housekeeper, gardener, another employee, or whomever, and tell them you can't both take the car in for repairs and also let in ABC's *20/20* camera crew for an interview at the same exact moment—something has to give.

I can recall an incident reported by a fellow assistant. Once, he was asked to drop the project he was working on so his employer's rented video could be returned to the local Blockbuster Video store *right now.* The assistant was in the middle of a major deadline and had to choose how to handle these demands. All the celebrity cared about was the video, so the assistant asked the celebrity to call the publicist who was waiting on the finished project and tell the publicist that the project would be delayed a few hours. Yes, he went the extra mile to cater to the celebrity, but if you must cater, at least cover your rear end!

New Thought: I express my desire to get the job done right, and if asked to drop one thing to handle something else, I let the boss know in very clear terms that Job A is now on the back burner because they want Job B done ASAP.

 # 3—Old Thought: Don't be different or show your emotions.

Be yourself. Laugh. Cry. Express anger when appropriate. Be joyful. Have admiration. Feel rotten. Be compassionate. Be willing to give a little. In other words, live life!

An assistant to a fashion designer called me in tears one night many years ago. She was in New York, and her celebrity employer was asleep in the other room. The assistant came to work every day at ten a.m. sharp where she interacted with the business manager, agent, and other staff members, and the designer slept in until six p.m. every day. Upon rising, the celebrity would then expect the assistant to be there until midnight to handle her duties—which, by the way, included going out to Taco Bell for snacks at ten p.m.! They made all the rounds of all the parties, and then the celebrity would come back to the hotel and sleep. But, of course, the assistant was expected to return on time early the next day, no matter how late they got in. (This is a big issue with 24/7 celebrities. They demand you kept their lives in order even when you are not there. Then when they DO arrive, they expect you to be there also.)These types of long hours are, unfortunately, common. Often employers expect the employee to just go with the flow and do their work without showing any sort of emotion, even though the employee may disagree with how something is done, or may want to express concerns about something or other.

The assistant was afraid to ask for shorter hours or show her employer that she too was exhausted! After a week of this, she was ready to quit. My advice to her was to either speak up or get on the next airplane out of there.

I said, "Sarah, why are you working in this kind of environment?"

"Well, it's my job, and I am afraid to leave or I won't get a recommendation," she replied.

"Is feeling used and stomped on worth a recommendation letter?" I asked.

"I guess not," she said, hesitantly.

I tried to speak to her as calmly as I could. "Sarah, if this behavior continues, you need to put your foot down. You need to tell your employer what you're feeling. Meanwhile I want you to take a serious look at how you got into this situation in the first place. My guess is that you were desperate to take any job you could, and that's how you landed here."

"Yes," she meekly replied.

"Well, that's never a good enough reason to take a job—ever!" I said. "So get out of there! I promise you another job is waiting for you back in Los Angeles."

I never heard back from Sarah as to how she left that job, but she did leave.

New Thought: I am who I am, and I stand up for myself and what I believe to be right!!

 # 4—Old Thought: Make a mistake and you'll pay for it.

Mistakes are a normal part of life, and you *will* make some mistakes in any job. But, what's the worst thing that can happen if do make a mistake and you tell the truth? My advice is, if you do something wrong—break something, double-book an auditorium, or simply forget an item on the list—tell your employer immediately and ask for help to fix the situation. In baseball, a player is considered a good player if he has a batting average of .333—that's an average of hitting the ball less than four times out of ten tries at bat! It's not ten out of ten. If you do something wrong, don't beat yourself up over it—give yourself a break.

A few years ago, my employer had a new personal chef whom we'll call Dana. Once, Dana borrowed the family car to go grocery shopping. I think she'd been on the job for only three days. While backing out of the garage, Dana scraped the left side of the car, creating a big dent. She came to me in tears, fearing for her life. I took her in to see our employer, Louise, and Louise's response was, "Well, now you've done this big mess up, so you don't have to worry anymore. Nothing you can do from now on will be this bad. No worries. The car can be repaired."

New Thought: Who I am is not determined solely by my successes and my failures, or by what I do right or wrong. Who I am is also determined by how I handle my successes and my failures.

 # 5—Old Thought: Never trust anyone. You'll be stabbed in the back some day.

Trust is a two-way street. Be trustworthy. Build a reputation for getting the job done by thinking ahead and being creative. At the same time, speak up and express the real you. You'll be promoting yourself and creating a strong working relationship with your boss and the people around you, just by being authentic. People will learn to count on you and rely on your confidence in them if you prove that you're trustworthy. It's good to establish friendships both inside and outside your industry or field of employment. It is healthy as well as smart to build many trusting relationships.

Maybe I've been doing my job too long, but I have to tell you that I love it when my boss introduces me to people as her "rock." The first time she went away on a long trip to Australia, I was left in charge of a huge remodel of her house. We had a new roof and new floors put in her home. The remodel was crazy, and when a gas leak was found in the roof above the kitchen stove two days before she was to return home, I admit I was a bit panicked. But, I was able to call in the proper people to handle the leak and still finish the entire job before she arrived.

You can be trustworthy with little things, too, not just with big projects. I remember one instance, around when my boss bought a home, which was built in the 1940s. Two days after she moved in, it poured so much rain that the roof and a window began to leak (this was before the new roof, mentioned earlier, was installed). The employer's home was in San Diego, and my home was forty miles north of hers.

I received a call that went something like this: "I have a leak in my roof, and the window in the front entryway," my boss said to me.

"Okay," I replied.

"But my neighbor next door has a roofing guy that we can call, and they can come out immediately. At least he can cover the roof to prevent the leak getting in the house."

"Great," I said.

"Here's the number. His office is amazingly only about one mile from my house!" she exclaimed. Then there was silence for a moment on the phone from my end.

I spoke again. "Um? Okay. I will call him," I said. I called the roofer, who showed up at her house promptly—within the hour, in fact. My question later was, why did I have to call the guy who was one mile from her house when she could've done it herself? That was just one of those "diva moments." But the moral of the story is, it did me no harm to handle such a small task for her. In fact, it made her trust me even more. Going the extra mile absolutely helps form a trust-based relationship.

New Thought: I can be counted on.

Those are some ideas about how to begin to change your working environment. If you are having difficulty with the old credos, try the following new thoughts for a week or so instead. To change the mantra "it's all about you, the employer," to "it's all about me, the employee," don't focus on the boss and give all your power away to him or her. You *can* stand up for yourself, make your feelings known, live without fear of mistakes, and trust yourself to gain the trust of your employer!

Chapter Four
Be a L.A.R.K.

To make changes in your life, you have to be a L.A.R.K. and start flying. Here's what L.A.R.K. means:

L—*Listen* to what is coming out of your mouth at all times.

A—*Ask* for what you want. ***Accept*** that you deserve it. Speak up!

R—*Relax* and think about things other than work. Laughter is good!

K—*Kick* old habits. ***Keep*** on going, no matter what. ***Keep*** your sense of humor. And above all else, be ***kind*** to yourself.

Let's break it down further:

L Is for Listen

Listen to what's coming out of your mouth. Quite literally, we shape the quality of our lives and the daily job routine by what we say. Are you actually listening to what you're saying?

"I hate my old, beat-up car."

"I don't like my nose."

"I can't stand my boss's wife."

"I never have any money."
"Mondays suck."
"I deserve a raise, damn it."
"They owe me!"

Begin to notice the way your day is going based on your use of negative self-talk. The old saying, "When it rains, it pours," really applies here. If you could tape record your conversations for even just one hour, you might be shocked at your responses to the people and events around you. At times they don't even give a second thought to what they are saying.

Try this for one week: listen for at least one hour a day to not only what you are saying but to what *others* are saying. You may be amazed to discover how many people seem happy and how many seem unhappy. There's a good chance most everyone is unhappy at least some of the time.

I'm sure you're thinking at this point, everyone I know is unhappy so who cares? Maybe they are. But you're not responsible for anyone else's life. You're only responsible for your life. However, criticizing yourself or others, being judgmental, acting irresponsible with your words—these are all things that can be damaging to you in the workplace, as well as in your personal life.

When I first began working in the entertainment industry at Capitol-EMI Records I used to see the people who worked in the Artist and Repertoire Department (A & R) come into work looking very world-weary. A & R was, and still is, considered the coolest department at a record company to be in. Everyone is so overworked. They have great horror stories about working with crazy musicians. They have to stay up late and work long hours because they are often out at clubs checking out new bands. It's unfortunate, but many people in the workplace love to complain about how bad they have it and how awful life is, even though they actually love doing their jobs. For instance, A&R people often go to concerts free of charge, which is a terrific way to hear new bands and even establish new bands. But the next day, all they can do is complain about how tired they are because they were out all night!

Someone using my L.A.R.K. method would immediately notice (by using the Listen technique) that complaining about having a good time is contradictory.

All habits *can* be changed. We're talking baby steps here. You may find it daunting to try to change your thoughts and habits overnight. Take it one step at a time. No one is asking you to do this all in one day! Be gentle with yourself. You're learning something new.

Do the listening exercise for a week. This may seem very foreign to most people, or very easy to others. After even just one day, you'll be able to tell where your listening and speaking skills stand on the seesaw. I promise you *will* see (or hear) a difference.

A Is for Ask and Accept

The next step in the L.A.R.K. method is to *ask* for and *accept* that you deserve what you want. This step is more difficult for most people than the listening exercise. Asking for what we want from our bosses (or lovers, or families, or mechanics) is a big step for many of us. Another step in the process is the realization that we actually deserve to ask for something and receive it. Talking with fellow personal assistants, I've found that they find this step to be very difficult to do. Asking for help, or asking for something like a day off from work or a raise, is torture to them.

If we pick our moments and don't rehash the past or act out of resentment or resignation, we can ask for what we want and actually get it. I've done it, and the ceiling didn't cave in on top of me. Like anything else, it just takes practice. We've spent so many years practicing being disappointed that it just takes a few times of being told *yes* before we start to believe we *can* have what we want. It really is that simple. Here's an example:

Assistant: "I'd like to talk to you about scheduling my vacation time this summer."

Boss: "I'm too busy right now. Just send me an e-mail."

Assistant: "I'll follow up with an e-mail so we have it in writing. And I'd like to confirm with you now that taking the week of July 4th off is all right."

Boss: "I'm going to be on Leno that week, right?"

Assistant: "Yes, Leno's people have confirmed, and I've already got your travel arrangements made. I need to make my own reservations so can you give me an okay on my days off?"

Boss: "As long as my stuff is set, that's fine."

Assistant: "Great! I'll follow up with you by e-mail and make sure you have everything you need before I leave the office on the third."

Using the L.A.R.K method, we're retraining our mind to accept the new thoughts as true. I knew an assistant who literally had to stand up every day to eat her lunch. She didn't have a real lunch break! She sorted the daily mail in mail slots (she worked on a large estate), and the only time she was "allowed" to eat was for that half hour while she sorted the mail. Asking to have a lunch break was too scary a thought for her, so she never did. I think she was in that job for five years before she finally left—that's a lot of lunches. Was it worth it?

R Is for Relax

R is for *relax*. A job can go more smoothly if we let things fall off our backs with ease and grace. Work really can be fun. But if we instead dwell on blame, shame, resentment, or anger, it's hard to find the humor in life and work. We need to play more in our workdays. Start with a hobby or something that makes you happy and focus on that. I suggest starting small. Take a walk at lunchtime, or buy a magazine that you normally wouldn't buy at work and read it cover to cover without interruption. Once you discover that the world isn't crumbling around you because you took a few minutes off, then aim for higher rewards. This may seem like a minor irritation—to actually have to think about yourself and not work—but it's very therapeutic to direct one's attention to something other than work for a few minutes every day.

For the past eighteen years, I've lived and worked only a few miles from the Pacific Ocean. I can count on one hand the number of times I've actually been to the ocean and walked on the sand, let my feet get wet, and had my face feel the sun beating down on it. While writing this book, I resolved to take a small step toward appreciating my proximity to this beautiful environment, and now I regularly drive to the ocean and sit and look at it, feeling the breeze and watching the sunset. I also recently moved a few blocks across from the ocean and enjoy that breeze every morning when I wake up and open my window!

It seems like a smart idea, in theory, to take time for ourselves, but over time we actually have talked ourselves into believing *no pain, no gain.* We're of no help to anyone if we don't take care of ourselves. Take up line dancing, cooking, needlepoint, bowling, or whatever. Do something *else* other than just work. One of my newest passions is the sudoku puzzles in the newspaper. I'm not very good at them, but it's a nice diversion. Everyone needs a diversion once in a while—make sure you don't deprive yourself of yours.

K Is for Kindness

Finally, the L.A.R.K. ends with K for *kindness, keep* going, *kick* old habits, and *keep* laughing. All of the above will keep the L.A.R.K. flying!

Kindness is sometimes tough to find in the working world, especially if you work in a service industry, yet it's essential to your mental health and to the health of those around you. Instead of the old saying: "Kill them with kindness," I rather like, "Keep them alive with kindness." Try this turnabout on the old phrase and you'll find yourself starting to kick the old habits of putting yourself and others down with your words and actions.

If you truly love what you're doing, I believe the universe will bring to you people to share the laughter with. People will show up in your life to support you in kicking habits, if need be. I used to be terrible about doing some kind of daily exercise. I have a wonderful friend, Marcie, who lives on a golf course. Every night she walks around this course (the trail is about a mile long!), at dusk. If you've ever been on a golf course, you know that the surroundings are beautiful, with old trees, little ponds, and flowers everywhere.

Marcie has been my support in making sure I kick the habit of laziness and making me take that walk with her at least once a week. I highly encourage you to enlist people to help you in the areas that you need the most work. Actually, my walks with Marcie cover all the areas of this part of the L.A.R.K.: I keep going, no matter what; kick the habit of being lazy; keep laughing as we talk on the walk; and I know I've been kind to myself by spending time with my friend and taking care of myself.

If you would like to see if you are using any or all of the L.A.R.K. ideas now, turn to page 49 for my little quiz.

Let's review the L.A.R.K. "steps to a new you":

- ***Listen*** to what you're saying and what people around you are saying. Try to only say nice things for an entire week. You can do it!
- ***Ask*** for what you want in life, and accept and expect that you deserve good things and that they will come to you.
- ***Relax*** and take your mind off of that which is troubling you. Do you have a hobby? Watch a funny movie. Go bowling. Take a walk with a friend. Don't take everything so seriously! What brings you joy?
- ***Keep*** on trucking but do it with grace, humor, and kindness. Especially remember to be kind to yourself. Don't be so hard on yourself. Start flying!

◆ ◆ ◆

When I began writing this little book four years ago, I showed the first few pages to fellow celebrity personal assistant, Gary Potter. He enjoyed reading about the seesaw but asked why I hadn't placed a fulcrum in the middle of the seesaw to balance everything out.

Gary's a lot smarter than I thought he was! He figured out what the purpose of this book is: a fulcrum is the leverage, or axis, you need to make the seesaw stabilize. The seesaw fulcrum is really *you* and your thoughts and actions. Only *you*, and no one else, can determine which way the seesaw of your life goes. You can stay a victim of your job, or you can be the magnificent L.A.R.K. I know you are. It's your choice. I hope you stop and smell the roses. You deserve the whole bouquet!

Part Two

Letters to Miss Know-It-All, advice columnist for the "stars behind the stars"

Naturally, as I began to be asked by other celebrity personal assistants about ways in which to improve one's working environment, the next logical step was to encourage people to send me their questions—anonymously if they wished—and I would reply in a forum that wasn't threatening. I hoped this would inspire other personal assistants to use the information to better their lives.

In the fall of 2001, "Miss Know-It-All" began. This was an advice column for *The Right Hand*, a now-defunct monthly publication for the members of the Association of Celebrity Personal Assistants. (The column also briefly appeared in *Wise* magazine.) The majority of my readers asked questions about the world of celebrity personal assisting, and I noticed that the more I answered their letters, the more I felt confident answering any question on any subject. Hence the pretentious title, Miss Know-It-All.

May you enjoy the letters that follow, all of which are completely real. Every letter listed here (except the one at the end, which was from a college student) was a question from an actual celebrity personal assistant made to me through my column. As you read the questions, you'll see why people wished to remain anonymous because the issues they were dealing with range from the ridiculous to the very serious.

From the desk of
Miss Know-It-All

Dear Miss Know-It-All,

I don't seem to be going anywhere in my job. I've been here for three years, and with no results. What should I do?

Stuck in a Rut

Dear Stuck,

Change careers? Flip burgers? Just kidding. Look at what makes you happy. Are you waking up every morning saying, "I love my life," or do you moan and groan? Watch how you feel and what you say during the day. What you give out is what you'll get back, baby. You can change your career if you wish, but if you don't change your thoughts about your job, you'll just keep repeating the same patterns no matter where you go.

Using the Listen segment of the L.A.R.K. method could help you here. Listen to what messages you're giving yourself. Are you telling yourself that you don't deserve anything better? Are you complaining to your friend about your work, but doing nothing to change your circumstances? Listening to what you say can influence what you think, and that energy is what goes out and comes back to you.

Keep the faith and say: *I greet my day with open arms.*

Miss Know-It-All

From the desk of
Miss Know-It-All

Dear Miss Know-It-All,

My boss is always trying to micro-manage everything I do. Help!

He's Driving Me Crazy

Dear Driving,

Give him a micro*phone* and tell him to talk to you all he wants … you'll get back to him. Okay, okay. Besides that idea, I suggest you talk to him and tell him you're a fabulous assistant who serves him well and he needs to trust you to do your job. You wouldn't still be there all these years later if that wasn't so. Ask him why he hovers over you so much. Perhaps he has lack of confidence and self-esteem issues? That would explain his over-the-top behavior.

By using the Ask segment of the L.A.R.K. method, you'll be showing your boss that you can think for yourself. You might be able to give him regular status update reports to reassure him that you're on top of things.

Affirm every day before you go to work: *My reality is mine to choose. I choose to be calm in the face of chaos.*

Miss Know-It-All

From the desk of
Miss Know-It-All

Dear Miss Know-It-All,

My boss has a new significant other that is driving me crazy. How do I handle someone coming into my space, where once there were two (just me and the boss) and now there are three?

Three's A Crowd

Dear Three's A Crowd,

Let's face it, a full-time job and an employer equals a marriage. Usually you both see more of each other than you do your own families. That's part of the appeal of the job. And one of your jobs is to be a shield to the outside world, and also to be a confidant.

The solution uses two segments of the L.A.R.K. method: Listen and Ask.

First, listen to yourself to find why you're having these feelings. So, you have to look at why you're angry. Is it because this other person is taking your boss away from you? That could be a jealousy issue. If so, you need to look at where you're getting your emotional support in your life. Is it 100 percent from your boss? Or is it 50 percent at work, 50 percent at home? If it's the former, then you need to look at why.

Even if you're afraid to say to your boss, "I'm mad as hell and I can't take it anymore!" (I loved the movie *Network*!), do it anyway. I can tell you from my personal experience that the more you do things you are afraid to do in *all* areas of your life, the more life will reflect back to you what you really want, not the other junk. It gets easier and easier every time you take that step. Each time you define clearly what you want, that trait shows up in your boss or your relationship or your world of money—whatever.

The second segment is Ask. You may have to ask for reasonable limits and expectations about your job duties. Clearly, if you were hired to support one person and if you're now expected to work for two, asking for compensation is reasonable. As for this other person at work muscling in on your empire, if it gets out of hand, sit your boss down and tell your him or her that you need to double your salary because now you're working for two divas, not one. That will get his or her attention, I promise.

Miss Know-It-All

From the desk of
Miss Know-It-All

Dear Miss Know-It-All,

I work for a movie star and my friends are always pestering me for autographs or insider tips on what my boss is doing. Frankly, I'm getting tired of them and just want to do my job without all that commotion. How do I get my friends to stop hassling me?

Bugged in Hollywood

Dear Bugged,

Working for a celebrity is a two-edged sword, isn't it? On the one hand, you probably like to be regarded as the one brilliant human being (out of all the people on the planet) that was chosen to work for this star. This, of course, makes you extra desirable as a friend. I mean, just standing *next* to you is an honor and a privilege. And if you can toss a cool story or two your friends' way, eureka!

Okay, that's laying it on a little thick. But that is part of the appeal of the job: both for you and for the "outsiders." The other edge of the sword is that you have to actually live your life. Suddenly your quiet existence is topsy-turvy. But it doesn't have to be.

For this dilemma, the Keep segment of the L.A.R.K. method can work for you. You can keep your friends by being honest with them about your limits. You can be kind in expressing this, and still be clear. The key is for you to be straightforward with your friends. You need to let them know that keeping your integrity on the job is more important than their friendship. If they are true friends, they'll understand.

Just tell yourself: *I have wonderful friends who support me in all areas of my life.*

Miss Know-It-All

From the desk of Miss Know-It-All

Dear Miss Know-It-All,

I have a problem I don't know how to solve. My boss has been great to me the last five years, always giving me a nice raise every year. But this year instead of the usual performance review where we sit down and talk about the past year and our goals, he just handed me a piece of scratch paper with my new salary on it and walked away. Not only was I shocked that he didn't take a moment to talk about it, but the raise was *half* of what I've received in the past.

Is he trying to tell me something or am I reading too much into the entire situation?

On the Way Down and Out

Dear on the Way,

On the way down and out? Not a good place to be putting yourself, my friend. There are two issues here to address. First, why, after five years with this person, are you worried about your job? Was there anything that you may have done in the past year to tick this person off? My guess is no, because if you did tick them off, they would've told you on the spot. No, my sense is that the boss had other things on his mind, and giving you a raise every year for five straight years feels like a routine to him by now. What a nice routine!

Which brings us to part two: perhaps you've become a little too complacent in your job, and both you and your employer need to take a moment to spend time reconnecting with each other. Working so closely with someone for all that time can become habitual, which can then become a bore for both of you.

L.A.R.K. logic will tell you to use the Ask method here. And instead of asking your boss, consider asking yourself some questions. I was going to suggest that you confront your boss and say, "What's up?" But I think that the smarter thing to do would be to confront yourself and your feelings of low self-esteem.

A raise every year for five years? There are other people out there in the workplace who would love to be in your shoes. Rejoice in your abundance. *Life is good!*

Miss Know-It-All

From the desk of
Miss Know-It-All

Dear Miss Know-It-All,

I'm fed up. My boss is unappreciative of how I got her on a fully booked, nonstop flight from New York to Bangladesh. She was unhappy that it was a 757, not a 747, and that the seats were blue and not maroon. Is she kidding? I am not making this up … it really happened!

Fed Up

Dear Fed Up,

This person has major issues that have nothing to do with planes, you know what I mean? The key thing you have to ask yourself here is: why is this job so important to me that I would still want to work for this person? Sometimes we count the votes, and sometimes we weigh the votes. So are you voting by gathering sympathy from everyone you know about this gal, or are you weighing your pros and cons?

Use the Listen segment of the L.A.R.K. method and ask yourself the questions above. What are you getting out of the situation? Besides a paycheck, is the drama and emotional angst fulfilling some part of your life that's empty? Is being able to one-up your friends with complaints about your boss part of the payoff?

If the boss is paying your rent and basically is your only source of income, you might want to hang around while you look for another job. But if you think you can get by on your own, I would get the heck out of there and chalk it up to the big "E"—no, not Ego … Experience.

Miss Know-It-All

From the desk of
Miss Know-It-All

Dear Miss Know-It-All,

I know people write you because they're unhappy with their jobs, but I actually like mine! My real question is, why don't I have enough time to write that novel? It seems by the time I'm done with work, it's all I can do to eat some dinner and go to bed.

Crunched for Time

Dear Crunched,

First of all, congratulations on enjoying your job. I like mine too! My guess is, because you like what you're doing, you gladly put in long hours or go the extra mile for your boss. It appears you don't have time for anything else but that's just an illusion—honest. Here's the real question to ask yourself: am I as passionate about writing that novel as I am about my day job? It's my experience that people with a passion about something find time to make it a part of their lives. So, are you willing to get up an hour early every day and sit in front of the computer, typewriter, or with a paper and pencil and write *something*?

For people with a passion, their passion is often their way of Relaxing. The L.A.R.K. method uses relaxation as a needed break to nourish your body, mind, and soul. If writing is your passionate relaxation, you'll feel inspired to work on your novel and it won't feel like work at all.

Years ago, I worked for the president of a major company. In his spare time, he'd written a highly successful novel, so he continued to get up at 5:00 a.m. every day without fail to write *something* on that paper before coming into work every day. Writing was his passion. Try this and let me know how things turn out for you.

Say every day: *there is plenty of time to get it done.*

Miss Know-It-All

From the desk of
Miss Know-It-All

Dear Miss Know-It-All,

My boss has been going though many highs and lows the past year (more so than normally!). I have accepted the volatile nature of the beast, but the past twelve months have been exceptionally more erratic. I believe that chemical substances are involved and are the primary reason for the mood swings. The mood swings are affecting our relationship as well as my ability to accomplish any level of work. What is my best course of direction—run or stay?

Moody on Melrose

Dear Moody,

This is a trick question with a trick answer. Option A: on the one hand, it appears you want to protect, care for, and yes, actually do your job for your boss. This means that you come to work every day and pretend nothing is going on. Option B: on the other hand, you don't want to be "the bad guy" who turns your boss over to the authorities for using, but you are genuinely worried about him or her. Should you contact someone? Option C: should you talk to him or her yourself?

You have a number of choices here. Is the solution A, B, or C? The answer: It's actually all of the above. Have you talked to the boss about your concerns? If you've been working for him or her for at least a year, your relationship should be one where you can have a straightforward conversation. If that isn't your relationship, write back to me and we'll cover that issue in another column.

Secondly, have you talked to his or her support group: wife, lover, best friend, parent or other relative, or agent? Do any of these people feel the same uneasiness that you do about the situation? They may have been waiting for someone (like you!) to say something. If more than one other person in the main "support" group agrees that there is a problem, you can formulate a plan together to get your employer help.

Using the L.A.R.K. method, by asking others what is going on with your boss, you can get a clearer picture of how to handle the issues involved.

Next, ask yourself some questions. Take a long, hard look at why you would come to work every day to a volatile environment. Are you a reactionary—allowing life to throw things in your way all day long for you to handle? Or can you grasp the concept of being a powerful creator of this magnificent universe that you live in? If you're a creator, then how did you get here? Now *that*, my friend, is the trick question!

And once you're done asking questions, listen to yourself in the same way you listened to the others involved with your boss. After listening, then act!

Miss Know-It-All

From the desk of
Miss Know-It-All

Dear Miss Know-It-All,

I'm so tired of being out of work! I never seem to stay in my jobs for very long. What can I do in the interview process to get a job and keep it?

Looking for Work

Dear Looking,

When you go to an interview, what's your attitude or preconceived notion about the employer (or yourself)? Often, we get sucked into everyone else's idea of the industry and of jobs. Don't listen when friends tell you stuff like, "all celebrities are egomaniacs," "all directors and producers abuse people," "you'll work an eighty-plus-hour week and the pay is lousy," "you don't have enough work experience," and, "no one will care about you and your needs." Believe me when I tell you that the celebrity I currently work for doesn't fit any of those molds. Such employers do exist … honest!

Before you ever get to the interview process, you need to be clear about what you want. Nothing is more important than your needs. When you get into the interview, come from the place of interviewing the employer. What are *they* going to do for *you*?

Using the L.A.R.K. method, listen to the employer's answers. What are they saying to you about hours, responsibilities, pay, time off, etc.? And follow up with questions of your own: ask about what's important to you.

I think it's only natural that personal assistants to celebrities want to be perceived as being caring, nurturing, kick-ass-efficient confidantes that the celebrity can't live without. All true. The part we, as assistants, seem to forget from time to time is that the most important person in the entertainment industry isn't the employer—it's *you.* Whoa. That's a revolutionary concept.

Post this on your refrigerator, in your car, on the bathroom mirror: *The most important person in the entertainment industry is me.* Take that attitude into your next interview and see what happens!

Miss Know-It-All

From the desk of
Miss Know-It-All

Dear Miss Know-It-All,

I have a question about getting a job. I'm nineteen years old and in my first year of college. When I look for work, I'm told I need experience first before they will hire me, but I need a job so I can have that experience. It all just seems like a vicious cycle to me. Help!

Looking for Work

Dear Looking,

But you do have experience—nineteen years' worth. Here's the deal: you need to go to the library and take out some books on how to write a résumé. Then write one from the perspective of what your existing skills are. That's all an employer really cares about. In other words, you're in college now, which means you finished high school, right? So to get through high school you had to be responsible, show up every day on time, complete the work assigned by a deadline, dress appropriately, interact with others, be part of a team to finish projects, and so on. Do you see what I'm getting at? All of those attributes are positive, and they're all useful in the everyday workplace.

Many adults way older than you struggle all the time with handling those responsibilities! They moan and groan about not being able to work with others, or they don't like deadlines, or they are constantly late to work. Whatever.

You have an edge over the rest of us old fogies (okay, okay, I'm just speaking about myself and not anyone else) because you have the fresh blush of youth on your side. Once you get that interview, be enthusiastic, and don't be afraid to brag about your accomplishments (like playing for four years in the high school band, or winning a scholarship to college). Then you'll be in charge and daring them to hire you.

It's time use the L.A.R.K. method for yourself and Ask for the job. You can do this literally at interview's end by saying, "What can I do right now to get this job?" Or you can do it more subtly with your follow-up thank-you notes and your can-do demeanor. L.A.R.K. methods work in all phases of employment, from job-hunting to job-leaving.

Say to yourself: *I deserve to have a wonderful job where I am respected and well paid.*

Miss Know-It-All

The L.A.R.K. Quiz

Below are a few questions you can ask yourself to see if the L.A.R.K. method might help get your life back into balance. Circle the answer that applies to you.

1. Do you have a hard time getting out of bed in the morning because you dread going to work?

   a. Always

   b. Sometimes

   c. Never

2. At work, does someone else control your workflow most of the time?

   a. Always

   b. Sometimes

   c. Never

3. Does your boss demean your requests or ignore you when you ask for something?

   a. Always

b. Sometimes

c. Never

4. Do you say yes to your boss without thinking, and then find yourself scrambling around to meet deadlines or take care of your personal needs?

   a. Always

   b. Sometimes

   c. Never

5. Does working overtime cut into your personal time? Does it negatively impact your family life?

   a. Always

   b. Sometimes

   c. Never

6. Do you have any physical symptoms associated with stress—grinding your teeth, headaches, stomach problems—that might indicate you're trying to do too much?

   a. Always

   b. Sometimes

   c. Never

If you answered mostly A, then you probably already know that using the L.A.R.K. method could help you deal with your job. Try reviewing the method, and consider committing to baby steps—making one small change at a time. For example, turn down overtime if it cuts into plans you've already made, and let your boss know ahead of time that a particular time and date is already booked for you.

If you answered mostly B, then you have an inkling that things aren't going as well as you'd like. Let L.A.R.K. guide you, and pick one area of your job to work on. Maybe it will be as simple as turning off your cell phone when you're out of the office, or stopping to review your workload before automatically saying yes to another work project.

If you answered mostly C, then you probably have a good work environment. Remember to let L.A.R.K. guide you outside of the office. Relaxing and rejuvenating yourself makes you a better employee. Being kind to others, mentoring a young person, and continuing with your life's plan will let your lark fly!

Afterword

While I was writing this book, a wonderful book about celebrities (and the public's obsession with fame) was released by Houghton-Mifflin entitled *Fame Junkies*, written by Jake Halpern. The Association of Celebrity Personal Assistants was lucky enough to be featured in the book, taking up a whole chapter. I highly recommend it.

www.acpa-la.com

About the Author

Shelley Anderson is a native Californian. Offering sage advice as the Hollywood columnist Miss Know-It-All, she's also the personal assistant to self-help author Louise L. Hay, and was formerly president of the Association of Celebrity Personal Assistants (ACPA). Shelley lives in San Diego with her daughter, April Genet.

www.dealingwithdivas.com

978-0-595-43436-7
0-595-43436-3

2679502R00037

Printed in Great Britain
by Amazon.co.uk, Ltd.,
Marston Gate.